ARE YOU PRESENT?

DR. STACEY L. BULLUCK

Copyright © 2024 Dr. Stacey L. Bulluck

All rights reserved. This publication, or any part thereof, may not be reproduced in any form or by any means, including electronic, photographic, or mechanical, or by any sound recording system or by any device for storage and retrieval of information without the written permission of the copyright owner.

Dedicated to God.

With the capacity you give me, I will honor You. I will glorify You with all that You place in my kingdom storage center.

When humans push through opposition, it makes us stronger beings.

Contents

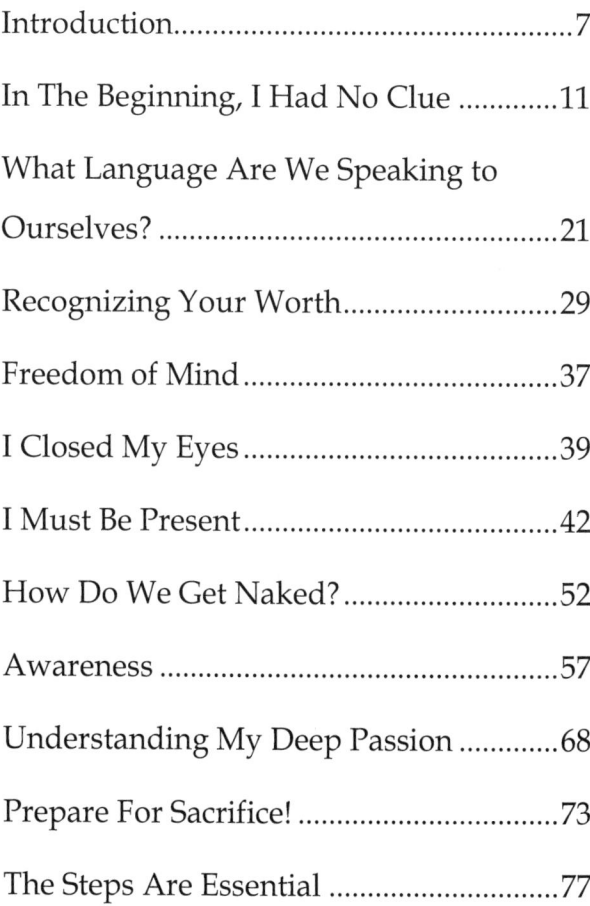

Introduction 7

In The Beginning, I Had No Clue 11

What Language Are We Speaking to
Ourselves? 21

Recognizing Your Worth 29

Freedom of Mind 37

I Closed My Eyes 39

I Must Be Present 42

How Do We Get Naked? 52

Awareness 57

Understanding My Deep Passion 68

Prepare For Sacrifice! 73

The Steps Are Essential 77

How to Break Habits That Create Obscurity In Your Vision and Fog Up Your Awareness 82

What is the Process? 87

Willingness 95

Acknowledgment 100

Adjustments 106

Alignments 110

Introduction

Have you ever wanted to know something so bad that you could physically feel the tug on your soul? That is how I feel when I sit down to write. Or more commonly known to me as "let's go talk to the people." I will never forget the first day God said to me, "Just go talk to the people through writing." It gave me clarity in my heart and soul, allowing me to gain deeper insight into how to express my true self. The authentic me feels at peace and overwhelmed at the same time. Yes, it is possible to have peace and be delightfully nervous because, usually, when the feeling of awareness hits, many emotions can flood our thoughts. Ideally, when this happens, our ego functions at a high capacity, and we can discern the direction we are motivated to go.

You know, the ego, according to Freud, "is the part of your personality that keeps you grounded." This grounding is necessary from the beginning if we desire to move toward a heightened place of awareness of who we are. It can be a scary place. We are noticing, identifying, and even observing our genuine, undisputed origin, coming into a deeper knowing of our best attributes. We all have qualities and features that are distinctive to who we are. Take a singer, artist, or musician, for instance. They may walk around singing or drumming on objects all the time. Someone who writes may be extremely descriptive in their choice of words when conversing. Perhaps they may even be called "loquacious." In other words, longwinded.

This discovery opens wells of emotions, and if we are not careful, it could turn into something uncontrollable. For some, having this sense of awareness could inflate what is known as *the id* because this state of presence expands our life and impacts where we trod. Understanding your own presence comes with power and strength that can be life-altering. Power and strength should not mean insolence and arrogance. However, notoriety can cause the mind to exaggerate the actual sense of being.

The awareness of our presence should only bring peace and love, with the sole intent of unlocking our power to manifest positive outcomes in life. Our outcomes are better because we become better decision-makers. Our self-confidence is through the roof, and as a result, we communicate clearly and intentionally. The perspective of our understanding is broadened in thought. We are no longer bound by our skewed assumptions and biases. Freedom of mind is a wonderful thing.

To accomplish a constant state of mind freedom, we must train our thoughts to agree with the inherent qualities already established in us, building on their strengths every day using our own voice of how we speak to develop a solid foundation for growth.

In The Beginning, I Had No Clue

Purpose will cause you pain. Growing pains are felt differently by everyone. I must admit that when I think of writing, a surge of emotions arises. There are moments when I am enthusiastic about sharing my heart, and then there are times when I am figuring out what my heart is saying and navigating a new direction—these are growing pains. Activated faith will cause purpose to move you, and you do not know where you are moving to.

That happened to me in November 2018. God said, "you are moving." I had no clue at first what to think and did not want to say anything that would cloud my mind and distort my hearing. I surrendered to the voice and moved from the DMV, aka the District of Columbia, Maryland, and Virginia, to California. I had no idea what I was moving to; I just knew purpose said its time to move.

Now, my limbs—specifically my legs—have moved me to the laptop with keys, expecting to be touched with the sensitivity that will only produce words that express the movement of time. As a writer, my fingers move quickly and methodically over the keys. Tick, tick, tick. Formulating sentences and framing words that ignite the reader's soul and bring light to their path, guiding them beyond superficial identities, but laser beam focused on purpose.

At times, the tug to enter this space feels so overwhelmingly unreachable that I want to escape it. BUT (Believers Understanding Truth), when it's deeply rooted, and you made an undeniable commitment at some point, it just keeps tugging. For me, the pain it causes not to answer or not follow the tug will always overrule any possibility that I would resist the tug on my heart strings. However, I did not get here overnight; it takes commitment wrapped in all its binding power to answer the call.

This is the call to be used to help someone else navigate through toils and snares as we steer through our own inward battles. Everyone faces struggles and must persevere through them to emerge victorious. Whatever the fight was about was not a dominant force in our lives. It does not dictate how we feel. We let how we feel dictate what we do or do not do. Eventually, the pull of purpose wins. Why? When we fulfill the call for that moment, strength comes from it. The strength comes through the love we show ourselves as we give in to who we are created to be. Whatever it is we are created to be, it will always bring access to love.

First, we, the vehicle of creativity, feel the love as we believe and trust who we are. It should make you feel on top of the world. It is when we are not fulfilling our purpose that we become miserable, depressed, desensitized, and unwilling. Notice those things I mentioned; we can change them. Yes, at the beginning of this chapter, I said purpose will cause you pain. The pain of not doing it is far worse than the agitation and uneasiness that come when you receive directions or the unction to move, and you refuse to move because of fear. Use fear as a catalyst. Remember it's simply coming into agreement with purpose. You will find the flow is endless.

Every time we agree with our purpose, we grow. There are going to be moments of "I have no clue where I am going or what I am doing." This is when you know to stay the course. If you are starting a business, keep searching to find the next step of growth. If you cook, write, sing, organize, develop, and create anything, keep going to the next steps. If you are here and are seeking ways to produce from the inside to the outside, from invisible to tangible, there will always be ways to be better.

I wrote something a couple of years ago, and it says, "The power within you is limitless, BUT sometimes you have to go in deeper to the center of who you are and extract the gifts and talents within."

In moments of disturbance, fatigue, and anxiety, understand this is the time to go in and pull from your inner reserves. The creative flow needed is right there. I was transparent about my own experience: when I sat down today to write, I had no idea what I was about to be used to express through these keys. BUT as I went with the flow of purpose that led me to sit down, listen, touch, envision, and have a palatable desire with every tick, tick, tick of the keys, I found my way. #insertsmilehere.

Here I am, writing one of the chapters, and I feel amazing. I feel accomplished. No, this is not the end of the book, or books, for that matter, but I am so proud of myself. I am bringing this up to help us understand we must push through any desires to do the opposite of what we are called to. Do it in faith, believing and trusting that you will not go wrong when you are doing what you believe is right for you. Showing up as the best you is best for those around you.

Galatians 6:9 - And let us not get tired of doing what is right, for after a while, we will reap a harvest of blessings if we don't get discouraged and give up.

Hebrews 11:6 (New Testament for Everyone) - And without faith, it's impossible to please God; for those who come to worship God must believe that he really does exist and that he rewards those who seek him.

In moments when emotions threaten to overwhelm you, do not let your senses deactivate you. Remember what you must do to live in the abundance of love, light, and freedom of being who you truly are. We must keep moving forward, and often, what we do involves our senses. The awareness of our sensory faculty is key because this is where the switch to doing what is right lives. Speak to your sensory faculties and remind them that you will not get discouraged to the point of giving up. The truth is that we all encounter discouragement, but we must not become it. We cannot allow anything that causes us to lose confidence to take hold within us.

Galatians tells us not to give our minds permission to be discouraged because it leads to the end of our desire to fulfill our purpose. In challenging moments, our goal is to push ourselves into what I call my alternative lifestyle: Worship!

As Paul says in Romans, "Offer your bodies as a living sacrifice, holy and pleasing to God—this is your true and proper worship." When I worship God by doing what I am created to do, I use agitation to increase my faith. Sometimes, I even acknowledge that I am feeling stressed and say, "Wow, this is not a good feeling," but I understand that life's stressors are here to stay.

Oh yeah, please know life stressors are here to stay. HOWEVER, I know that when I bring my body, gifts, and talents and use them as tools that uplift, encourage, and enlighten others, all while believing and trusting what God gave me, I am deserving of it. As a result, we are rewarded with greater ability, power, and love to continue pushing through any opposition because the true reward is that we become stronger beings. Physical strength is valuable, but spiritual strength is unmatched.

What Language Are We Speaking to Ourselves?

Numerous studies have shown how our words affect our lives. Negative words have quietly become an everyday norm, framing worlds and shaping lives. It's time to change the narrative. Words are simply thoughts expressed, and once they are released, our bodies aren't savvy enough to discern which parts to accept and which to reject. As a result, we accept everything spoken, and the effects of those words will manifest somewhere in our lives—through our behavior, for example.

Let's discuss the language we use with

ourselves: is it empowering or disempowering? We must have the ability to empower ourselves. Yes, it's great when we can watch or listen to someone else, but that individual is not always accessible. I know, I know—in this age of technology, anyone with a message is just a touch of a screen or keyboard away. BUT (Believers Understanding Truth), it's our responsibility to encourage ourselves. Encouraging ourselves creates an internal bond that fosters trust.

There are times when we talk ourselves out of trusting who we are, but now is the time to change that. By the end of this book, I pray that you will have full trust in your ability to give yourself permission to achieve your goals and fulfill your dreams. The goal of the words on these pages is to support our continual growth and development. What we speak about becomes the main character in our beautiful story. Understand that every vision of prosperity you have is given to you for your benefit and those connected to you. Once we unlock the door that's blocking our permission, we will walk in full authority because we will believe we are equipped with the power, confidence, strength, and self-determination to handle this journey we call life.

Now, let's briefly examine disempowerment and why we must not allow it. Trust me, we won't linger here. Plain and simple: we must never again disrespect ourselves. We will no longer continuously insult, find fault, or criticize ourselves. While it's important to look for areas to improve or engage in self-introspection to become better—and yes, we should do this until the day we leave this earth—BUT (Believers Understanding Truth) know that we are eternal beings and will never stop growing in spirit. The choice is yours to grow or stay the same. In the flesh, yes, it has an expiration date. But when we are gone, if we have accomplished most of our life's mission and shared our gifts and talents, we will live on in our deeds.

No more perpetuating the lie that "sticks and stones may break my bones, but words will never hurt me." That was the biggest lie ever told to mankind. Words create feelings of sadness, anger, embarrassment, anxiety, helplessness, and the emotion of being alone. Emotional abuse is not a one-time thing.

Words, once spoken, strike the soul they attach to. They can hurt and often amplify our pain. These words remain forever in our unconscious, if not our conscious, memory. This explains why unresolved emotional issues manifest in various forms of negative behavior. The term often used is "triggered." When something activates what is attached to your soul, your body begins to express the associated emotion. It is our responsibility to manage these feelings as we develop emotional intelligence.

BUT we can also approach this from a positive perspective, which is why I am writing this and why you are reading it—to gain a positive outlook. We are now speaking the language of edification to ourselves and are no longer dependent on anyone else to define or express who we are to the world. We have taken full responsibility for being our own source of influence.

The Effect of a Soundwave: A Spoken Word

"Words, whether positive or negative, not only affect us on a deep psychological level but can also have a significant impact on the outcome of our lives. It has been found that the sound waves emitted when we speak not only carry the message spoken but also create an impact on the person at the receiving end. Sometimes, this impact lasts forever. If it's positive, it can boost a person's energy and self-esteem and bring out the best in them. If it's negative, it can negatively affect a person's sense of self and, ultimately, alter the direction of their lives."

If you were to hear a large blast right now, it may or may not startle you. However, I'm almost certain it will provoke some kind of reaction from you. The effect would be different for each of us. According to psychology counselor Carol Roach, everyone's brain is wired differently. Psychologists may categorize people's reactions by someone's emotional state. Now, I believe we all can control our emotional state. I did not say we can control what may happen to produce an emotional state, but once it happens with practice, we may use our own influence to control how we feel. We can govern ourselves. We do this by following this principle.

Romans 12:2 (Amplified Bible) - *And do not be conformed to this world [any longer with its superficial values and customs], but be [a]transformed and progressively changed [as you mature spiritually] by the renewing of your mind* *[focusing on godly values and ethical attitudes], so that you may prove [for yourselves] what the will of God is, that which is good and acceptable and perfect [in His plan and purpose for you].*

When we are willing to undergo a thorough transformation and commit to the process that leads to a permanent change in mindset, we realize the value we bring to this world.

Recognizing Your Worth

To recognize means to "know exactly," and to realize without having any discrepancy or deception about your worthiness will cause an escalation of thought regarding who you are. You will begin to accept your role in this world as the vehicle transporting riches from place to place because you are spiritual, capable, intelligent, and virtuous. You are a kingdom storage center.

***Proverbs 31:10** - An excellent woman [one who is spiritual, capable, intelligent, and virtuous], who is he who can find her? Her value is more precious than jewels and her worth is far above rubies or pearls.*

Note: The pronoun depicted here as "her" is descriptive of the house of God, and if the world crisis has taught us anything, it should have shown us the place of God's dwelling is not in brick and mortar—it is in us. God has placed capability and wisdom within us and given us the capacity to expand. We have the power to change everything we connect with for the better. When will you allow your behavior to reflect that of someone who knows their worth is far above any earthly jewel created? It is past time for us to grasp who we are fully. We are the dwelling place of God—a kingdom storage center.

James 1:17-18 *(The Message Translation)* — *So, my very dear friends, don't get thrown off course. Every desirable and beneficial gift comes out of heaven. The gifts are rivers of light* *cascading down from the Father of Light. There is nothing deceitful in God, nothing two-faced, nothing fickle. He brought us to life using the true Word, showing us off as the crown of all his creatures.*

God says, "You are worthy to be a crown created just for His glory." I can imagine us shining through all the circumstances we encounter along the way. There is no time to allow discouragement to win. It is time to trust and believe we are capable of BEING the best representations of God's crown, formed in greatness and power to accomplish our life's intended purpose as a spiritual being who can cultivate intelligent and good practices that lead to an enhanced life.

Spiritual Meaning

The meaning of being spiritual these days

has taken on such a vast perspective, but I want to clarify that it should not be considered spooky or religious. From my point of view, spirituality refers to someone who lives their daily life being guided by a force that is much greater than we are. As spiritual beings, the power within us provides all we need to live a life filled with Godly principles.

An example of this would be when we choose to do right or wrong. We choose to follow what is morally right because right sets us up for good, and wrong sets us up for failure. When I say right and wrong, this pertains to moments of quick judgment where the outcome may be good, but the action to get too good is wrong. Reads simple, right? I am chuckling here because when things seem simple, they often stem from what we cannot see, like through the thoughts entertained in our minds before the behavior is exposed.

In that space of time, we are given the opportunity of choice—between the thought and the action of the thought. Here is where we acknowledge we have the power of choice. The choice is made according to the certainty of our value. When we are confident of our significance, there is understanding. With knowledge, we recognize that some things are simply not at our level, and we decide with wisdom leading the way.

I could not think of a better way to help you understand your full value than to share the verse below. This snatched my heartstrings and immediately provided the insight needed to fully sum up who we are and how significant we are on Earth—ambassadors of riches. Especially when we choose to BE the distributor of these riches, surrendered to the marvelous spiritual being who is created in the likeness and image of greatness that is on display for all to see.

Psalm 139:13-16 (The Message Translation): "Oh yes, you shaped me first inside, then out; you formed me in my mother's womb. I thank you, High God—you're breathtaking! Body and soul, I am marvelously made! I worship in adoration—what a creation! You know me inside and out, you know every bone in my body; You know exactly how I was made, bit by bit, how I was sculpted from nothing into something. Like an open book, you watched me grow from conception to birth; all the stages of my life were spread out before you. The days of my life all prepared before I'd even lived one day."

Accept that you are great, regardless of some of the behaviors you have exhibited in the past that may not have been so wonderful. They are not a determination of who we are spiritually, nor do they determine the outcome of our lives. There is a reason why our physical growth was carefully monitored during our developmental process in the womb. From before the time of conception to our emergence, God saw you, you were in full view, and there is an expectation of who was being sculpted, some say knitting together. Joint by joint, piece by piece, you are the work of art that is cherished and loved — a masterpiece.

Now, our eyes are open, and our vision

becomes clearer with every new day. This will only turn out well when we are committed to continuing the process of recognizing and appreciating who we are. No more downplaying our own greatness. No more allowing our ideas to self-destruct in our own minds before they have an opportunity to develop and be displayed for all to see. We are worth it! Say it out loud: I AM WORTH IT!

Freedom of Mind

I am going to go out on a limb here and say that God wants to bring us to our original state—a state where our minds are free of clutter. Back to the original place, back to the state of mind when he placed us in Eden. Let us examine how to get to the place of constant flow. The place where our thoughts are free of biases and judgment from within. Back to a place where we revered ourselves as set apart to grow and expand in the riches of His glory. A place of pleasure and delight. The place given to humanity as a gift from God.

God gave Eden with the intent that humans

would always work to protect the gift given to them. Then, in turn, we would live free of things that would give us thoughts that we were not good enough to fulfill our life mission. To flow out of Eden. To continually live in an Eden state of mind. God originally intended for humanity to live in Eden and be at rest, knowing they would not want for anything ever. He gave us the freedom to flow — to Fully Live and Overtly Win (FLOW) consistently. We are set on a path that brings us into this keen awareness of who we are and learn to remain present to keep the same perpetual course of supernatural influence.

I Closed My Eyes

Poem

In moments of preparation to become this place of serenity and peace.

I just close my eyes, and the sun and wind usher me to a place of complete surrender.

A tranquility of untouched matter.

The water flow gently soothes my soul.

It seems I left this space to gain a grace so powerful that its force grips my soul.

I'm metamorphosized into expansion.

Stretching far beyond galaxies and stratospheric activity.

Changed, awake, and aware of this place that pours every ingredient needed for my life's growth.

And all I did was close my eyes.

My world became transformed. Mind resurfaced anew.

My goals, they grew too.

Unconsciously made conscious of me.

This sacred process of healing has turned into a state and physical feeling of insurmountable greatness, joy, and, most of all, love.

That's why it's so cool to be in love. The human soul is magnified in it. In its beauty to be present.

Are you present? Present for the unexpected awareness that is yours every day. Like the one that I'm writing about at the moment. A bird just walked right up to me. You see that peace we house will draw and provide a safe space. Humph providing a safe space. This is an unexpected awareness. All this is because of my desire to be prepared as a Sanctuary.

I Must Be Present

I'm so in love with God. I must be present. When God shows up and has something for you to do, will you be aware enough to hear, receive, and execute? Will you be like the two disciples Jesus instructed to "go and untie the donkey and her colt and bring them to him?" They were present physically and spiritually. They were able to hear the verbal request. God is still making verbal requests today. The spiritual part was that they were instrumental in fulfilling the word God spoke in *Zechariah 9:9 (Living Bible):* *"Rejoice greatly, O my people! Shout with joy! For look—your King is coming! He is the Righteous One, the Victor! Yet he is lowly, riding on a donkey's colt!"*

Like most humans, they probably wondered why the need for the donkey. In the story, there was provision made for the thoughts of where, what, and why. See, this is where we can make a mistake by asking too many questions. Let me be clear: I am not from the old school of "don't question God." It is necessary to ask questions, especially for direction. God says if we lack wisdom, we should ask Him.

Just the other day, I made a statement concerning the upward trajectory of my life and how I did not understand how I had reached this place of mega blessing. The very next day, God sent me an answer in John 13:7 - Jesus replied, "You don't understand now what I'm doing, but it will be clear enough to you later." The first two words alone made me stand in awe. "Jesus replied." See, I told you; you are worthy. When we are spiritually present, Jesus will reply. So, I say if you have a question, ask God. The answer may not be what you think or expect, BUT (Believers Understanding Truth) know without a doubt that there will be an answer.

The two disciples were given instructions to carry out the assignment. The job was to get the donkey, the vehicle, or transportation, if you will, for the King of Glory to ride into the city in the humblest way, displaying the symbol of peace to those who witnessed it and needed the visual to get an understanding. You know how human tendency can be, and I am thankful that there are times when God will accommodate our curiosity even though we may not recognize the magnitude of what we are seeing until the right time. Most likely, they were aware of the prophecy but did not expect to be used to fulfill it. Know that God wants to use us to complete the plan. God wants to use us to be participants in changing the world.

When we are aware of who we are and who we receive instructions from, there is little need for understanding. The New Testament disciple was not within earshot of the prophetic utterance from Zechariah. There are times when we are privileged to know all that will happen as we make our way to the pinnacle of life. However, know that the King has already put the things and people in place for you to reach your God-given position. BUT we must be present and available.

There are many times my work will require me to provide my dates and times of availability, and I will send the information to the requester. When God needs someone in the physical realm, will you be present? Will you be present and able to say, "Here I am. I am available?"

Will you be present when God shows up in the cool of day? Or will you hear a familiar sound that has now become distant to your ear?

God said, "Adam, where are you?" Adam's physical body was present, but his heart was not. Somehow, it had left, and now its attention was directed toward something else. That was his physical self. Looking at our humanness can cause us to become self-centered.

Self-centeredness makes us focus on the wrong areas of life. It makes us focus on things that do not matter, like body shape, size, and color. All things that are seen with the human eye. Human sight can be deceiving. There is evidence that has debunked the eyewitness theory and shown it is not the most reliable. Have you ever been in a situation where you knew you made a mistake? A big one at that. What was the first thing you wanted to do? Retreat! Withdraw, hide, and leave. Yes, we may remove ourselves from the situation at some point if possible. None of those are solutions to feelings. For feelings, you must face them head-on. It is impossible to get away from our feelings.

Let's take a little turn right here for a moment. I was speaking to someone about not being able to feel any emotions at all. I said, "It is good to feel our emotions; this way, we can deal with it." But we must make the choice to do so. I remember a time in my life when I did not feel, or should I say, I did not allow myself to feel; therefore, it was impossible to heal. BUT (Believers Understanding Truth) know that if we find our way to God's presence and get naked, allowing vulnerability to be our guide, God will not take advantage of our willingness to expose those areas in which we feel weak. God is made strong in our weakness. Wow, that just clicked. When we give God our weakness, it is no longer weak because God is all-powerful and all-knowing. God brings back to life the feeling and circulation of dreams, passions, and desires.

Okay, back to being able to feel. At the beginning of this awareness journey, the feelings (emotions) may be all over the place because you are entering into unknown territory — a place where we must face some hard truths about who we believe we are. These may be words that have pumped us up or torn us down. Either way, the sum of it is not accurate. Some of us have or had problems with vanity, while others struggle with low to no self-esteem. Neither are healthy tools for developing or improving our everyday lives. So, please understand this may not be the easiest thing to do, BUT (Believers Understanding Truth) know it is the best solution when you desire to live in freedom. Because where freedom is, there also is God's Spirit, giving us sound guidance and direction to a life of liberty to soar as high as we choose. This requires some shedding and removal of the fig leaf we are covering up with—a willingness to eliminate false righteousness and replace it with a pure heart. We must take this opportunity to rid ourselves of things that we make seem as if they are justifiable.

Now, remember that this is just an example; it is okay not to tell the whole story. For instance, you may be on your way home from work and decide to stop at a restaurant, but you don't tell your family or spouse you ran into an old fling, and the two of you had dinner together. Therefore, just because things turned out okay does not mean that when the full story is revealed, the other person will be okay with it because the information was hidden. Hiding flaws is never good. Being open, honest, and fully transparent — naked, if you will — is the best pattern to follow.

How Do We Get Naked?

How do we get naked, or in other words, how do we become vulnerable in the presence of God? We must be willing to take all defensive postures away. We must be willing to allow our shame and guilt to be exposed. Too many people are walking around carrying guilt and shame as if it is a part of their identity, believing they are the feeling. Yes, your behavior may be shaky right now because you don't trust yourself yet. You are in the phase of circulating thoughts again. There is nothing we can do about things already done. No one has the power to turn back the hands of time. So, you might as well let it go. If you are still holding on to things that have gotten too heavy and you have become numb to life, let go and start reading *"Don't Let Your Brain Go Numb: Regaining Power Through Resilience."* It will disrupt areas that continually feed you a false narrative. The book gives insight into what is going on and how to get energized again and want to get back to the place where God intended us to be — when we were not hiding.

God is attracted to the being we became when he blew the breath of life into dust. God recognizes the being He made happen. When we choose not to walk in the state of happening and instead hide who we are, God must call to the human part and get its attention for us to come back to His presence so he can have a conversation with us. This is when life begins to tap you on the shoulder. God is calling humans to bring us back to the place of being, to the place of awareness, where we are clear about the greatness we possess and not constantly focusing on our human flaws. Let's begin to walk with God daily.

When God shows up, a rest takes place, and all the distractions of humanity cease. It would be fantastic if we could find in us the willpower to carve out time to spend with God. When God walked with Adam and Eve in the cool of the day, that was a specified time. That was their time to get to know God, and the more they found out about God, the more they found out who they were. When we begin to discover the vitality and strength of who we are, it is necessary to expose those elements we want to hide, thinking they somehow benefit us.

You know, those little things like procrastination and adding undue stress by waiting until the last minute can cause you to feel you cannot fulfill purpose, but if we expose them, they can be dealt with and permanently resolved. Then, we can stop trying to hide things we think are not good enough to be seen. Everything about you is good enough to be seen and heard.

Being aware of who you are brings responsibility to "BE." Be alive, be viable—a capable resource for life. Having our heart, mind, and soul in a state of awareness about who we are is the only way to ensure we are "on point" in life. When we say "on point," the position is the most exposed in the military. Holding on to the past, to the person who did not believe in you, places a veil over the eyes of our hearts and makes us believe a myriad of things about ourselves—most of which do not make us feel deserving of the greatness we possess within. I want us to walk in total freedom today—liberation from all things that hide the authentic you. Walking in freedom just simply means we no longer allow our thoughts to enslave us to things that move us away from the genuine you.

We have a responsibility of presence. Once we become aware that there is something great about us, it is time to allow the process to happen. Do not try to alter, stop, or change the process. The gem is being created from the disturbances and disruptions in life, just like the process of nacre, where the irritant becomes a pearl.

Awareness

Some of us have had, or are currently experiencing, a break or interruption in our normal activities and processes. Allow awareness to guide you through whatever stage you're en route to becoming this flawless gem—a pearl that symbolizes purity. You see, the gem is not tangible; it resides in the heart of humanity. Oh, by the way, the pearl is the only gemstone that does not need any alteration by human hands. It comes out of the oyster shell as a treasure. So today, allow God to finish the process of becoming. Think of it as you are becoming a gem of a writer, a gem of an artist, a gem of a wife, mom, sister, or entrepreneur;

there are no limits. It is necessary to understand that it took time for the pearl to develop inside of the oyster. The crystallizing process takes time. The forming, gelling, setting, growing, and maturing process takes time. The rarer the gem, the longer the process.

Do not harshly judge yourself if you are not where you think you should be. I know there are those who are reading or listening to this book who have only tapped the surface of who they are. As Paul prayed, my prayer is the same as Ephesians 1:18 in the New Living Translation says, *"I pray that your hearts will be flooded with light so that you can understand the confident hope he has given to those he called — his holy people who are his rich and glorious inheritance."* God has called you — I know you hear it every time you do that thing that you love and maybe hate so much. This is the fear of success trying to creep in; do not let that happen. Yes, it's going to take work, but you are made with specific measurements to fit into your life position. May your awareness be genuine and your life be fully liberated to be you.

Numbers 6:26 NIV: The LORD turn his face toward you and give you peace.

When we truly come face to face with who we are, this is an opportunity for God to look at us through us and provide the peace that is needed. It's the peace that comes from the reassurance of knowing who you are. When we see who we were created to be, there is a peace that accompanies that understanding. Peace is the source needed to come to a place of complete surrender to who you are. Once we accept the responsibility of who we are, we can focus and achieve so much more because our concentration is no longer on the external image we see in the mirror. Instead, our attention is intentionally seeking what is inside of us that will give us the strength, will, and know-how to get us to our end goal.

A simple look in the mirror is a reminder that this is the face God is using. Being in an intimate state of intentional focus, God is looking at you, and you are looking to God as the unveiling of our vulnerable places becomes wide open. The world is beginning to see us, and we are beginning to see ourselves. This is the place where there is a possibility that we may be rejected for our authenticity. BUT (Believer Understanding Truth), our focus is on the face of God.

Everywhere we turn, we see God because our focus is clear. We receive daily instructions through our senses — through our ability to see the vision God is giving, to know when God speaks, to hear when God speaks, and to smell the aroma of God, recognizing when God is present. These attributes place us in a mindset of peace. We demonstrate peace when we are Persistent in Excellence, living in Abundance, and being Creatively Effective. These are the true ingredients of peace.

Here is the blessing of peace: being aware of the presence within and in your life keeps us persistently striving for excellence to live in abundance as we use our creative abilities to be effective on the earth. Effectively being who we are without hesitation or questioning. This means we are no longer questioning God about who He is or who we are in Him. In God, we learn how to freely live, freely move, and freely have our being.

Free living can only be accomplished when we are focused on the directions given to us. This is needed to make any changes in life and, more importantly, to make position changes as we grow in our process of life. The peace will keep us walking through perpetual God-opened doors if we shift when God shifts. We must move as one to have the continual flow of the breath of life breathed into us. God blew into man's nostrils. If we are not in the face of God, how does he blow where he created us to receive air? Taking in air through our nostrils activates what is called the parasympathetic nervous system. This system helps us to calm down. In other words, as the book of Numbers said, when God is looking towards us because we have made it our business to be in the face of God, it is then we can walk pleasantly and comfortably in the ways of God. Meaning we can flow in the presence of peace as we progress through life.

There are many levels of awareness. When life is shifting, we must be aware of the direction of the movement.

Are you ready to be aware?

The state of being aware of our own uniqueness and the abilities we possess leads us to our highest self. Reaching self-actualization is to get to the pinnacle of a season in our lives. I believe there are many things in our being that have great potential to be realized. My question is: do you want to cross over into a space of obscurity and unknown? Of course! Yes, along with all the enthusiasm I could express about it, even when my physical body, the human side of all of us, is not so convinced. BUT (Believers Understanding Truth) know the only way to push through the human is to simply just keep doing it. What is your it? I do not know, but here are some thoughts to encourage us to continue becoming more aware of who we are.

- Keep pushing past the nos.
- Never stop believing in your dream, product, or brand.
- Make sure your why is firm. It cannot be moved because it is attached to something bigger than you.

Awareness is what we need to explore to help us understand ourselves. Each person has distinctive characteristics that make them their authentic self, the soul of who they are. While serving in the military, I was a dental hygienist for a portion of my career, and one of my instructors told me something that had a major impact on how I looked at my worth and work. She said, "Always be willing to sign your name on the patient's record." My interpretation of that is: make sure your work is of a high standard, and you are proud to sign your name. You are proud to identify with it. It will make you think about how you go about what you do. I want to always be proud of who I am and the imprint I leave on the earth. We can only leave an identification mark when we are being. Being that is our ability to happen. It is our ability to make our mark and take our position on this journey, leaving evidence of our essence here.

Leaving evidence requires some inner workings to be done. Therefore, we must ask the deeper questions. This may take a moment to ponder and fully digest. Take some time and write out what comes to your mind. Awareness will force us to take off all masks. What is the state of who you are telling yourself you are?

This is the number one key to successfully being you. No one on this earth can give you a clear, heart-pounding vision of who you are. This responsibility is solely dependent upon the individual. Know what you want out of life. Know what you will and will not accept as your normal. You have the power and the right to be the best at being you.

Understanding My Deep Passion

What part of your being distinguishes you from others? What is your automatic action?

What makes you essential? For me, I know I am vital as a human being, and I'm equipped to assist others in seeing their potential. I'm working with a young lady who wants to cook for the homeless. We helped her do that weekly for three years.

Awareness brings understanding. There are many times in life when I have no clue what is going on. However, I am fully aware of who I am and that I have the capacity to BE.

I am confident you either have or are coming into full awareness. Why do I write this with certainty? It is simple because you are reading this book, and my purpose for writing it is to reach people who desire to be alert in their minds — seeking to have clarity and understanding about this thing called life. This is a time of passion unveiling and unraveling the mysteries. I have a deep passion for helping others.

One of the groups I am helping is my Veteran sisters, who have been incarcerated. There are many days I wonder why I am so passionate about helping and serving. Now, I no longer want to know why the passion is here. I just follow, and it has led me to some wonderful places. Now, I seek to understand what it will take to pursue this passion. Who are the players that need to be involved? Of course, the women, but how do I get to them, and when I do, what should I bring to them? In other words, how am I able to effectively serve them?

This passion was revealed to me at a difficult time in my life. It was after my eighteen-year military career ended due to injury. To this day, I still do not remember when or how I met the Chaplain at the Anne Arundel County Detention Center. This divine meeting came during a space of emptiness. BUT (Believers Understanding Truth) know that it was the perfect storm. When discovering your passion, it is not necessary to try and figure out why it is here. It is the moment in time to understand — to gain knowledge. I am sure the artist Picasso took time to understand paint and the art of painting. It is obvious he was gifted at painting, but I am sure there were instances when colors began to bleed into one another and began to take on different shades and hues. I am feeling happy at the thought of seeing something as a new color. Imagine something you do is a new phenomenon. Yes, believe it. Just like with many artists, scientists, trainers, teachers, musicians, and I could go on and on and on, new knowledge is revealed to you, and you are the one who is chosen to bring it to the world. Oh, I am excited. I hope you are too. Excited to now unlock your deep passion and bring something to the world. See, the part you bring will make the world you touch a better place. Glory BE To God!!!

To have a deep, all-consuming feeling about being your greatest self is what you need. It drives you to do everything possible to achieve your goal. There must be an internal will that propels you forward and energizes you to push through regardless of obstacles or setbacks.

Prepare For Sacrifice!

Prepare for sacrifice in the moments of preparation to become this place of serenity and peace. It will require a full surrender. Here is where I want to bring what I call a peaceful sacrifice to your attention. This is a state of mind to live in a place of discovery. Discoveries propel us into the action of being. Realizing the gateway to being requires us to intentionally annihilate our way of doing and thinking, desiring to live free of self.

I wish you were here to witness the curvature of my lips and this radiant smile because as I write these words, the light that floods my soul makes me want to come into a much greater awareness of who I am. I pray you can feel it even more as you digest these words—willingly wanting to be in a state of mind where you can no longer deny who you are. Think of a world-class athlete; there is no repudiating the evidence they are living proof; they believe who they are. I am asking God to turn on the floodlights so you will not miss seeing who you are. That you will embrace you and, in your acceptance, you fall so deeply in love that you will never again lose sight of who you are.

Getting to that place requires sacrifice. It is not a painful sacrifice but a peaceful surrender of your human will as you yearn for the hope of the call of the Spirit to be the evidence of the divine guarantee. Now, you are in sync with the confident expectation and divine guarantee. Why are you able to move in peace and stay continually in a state of rest? Because you know this greatness within you is immeasurable and unlimited. There is no stopping you because you are peacefully aware. Even when life shows you another side, it cannot shake your trust because your dependence is not in your physical body, BUT (Believers Understanding Truth), depend on the knowing and on the experience you have, and your experience produces confidence. Every time you feel this conviction, remember it as a point of reference, time after time, because life is going to try you. This is why all distrust and skepticism must be met with firm hope. Always ALLOW (Always Let Love Overcome Wantonness) God's power rest rules and abides in us, and we will not fulfill the gestures of the flesh, BUT

(Believers Understanding Truth) will actively work in the strength of God Almighty.

Ephesians 1:18-19 (Amplified Bible) - *18 And [I pray] that the eyes of your heart [the very center and core of your being] may be enlightened [flooded with light by the Holy Spirit], so that you will know and cherish the [a]hope [the divine guarantee, the confident expectation] to which He has called you, the riches of His glorious inheritance in the [b]saints (God's people), 19 and [so that you will begin to know] what the immeasurable and unlimited and surpassing greatness of His [active, spiritual] power is in us who believe. These are in accordance with the working of His mighty strength…*

The Steps Are Essential

I know that sounds simple. There are times when we may be in a mood of grandeur and tell ourselves we are able to accomplish something when we are just learning this new facet of who we are. Yes, you have dreamed of it many times, and now you are making strides toward reaching the goal of mastering your craft, but you are in the beginning stages. Therefore, it's not advantageous for you or the person you want to please to go into some form of expectation when currently you are learning to be proficient. Awareness of our capabilities during moments of grandeur is necessary for navigating effectively. Remember, we are all heading in a direction, and because you are reading this book, you are well on your way to developing yourself.

For us to be in a constant space of aggrandization and elevated power, we must constantly be aware of what season we are in. We all have seasons and phases, much like the moon. BUT we must learn to be like the moon and follow its pattern. Although the moon finds itself in different stages, the moon still shows up every night, never missing its moment to shine. Some nights, it shines brighter and looks bigger. When I was writing this, it was a week after daylight savings time, and just like creation does, it teaches, and we humans desiring to BE must change positions. Just like the earth we were created from, we were transformed to align with the shift, so it is necessary for us to learn from creation. The Creator is shifting the earth; now is the time for a position change. When we become keenly aware of our seasons and discern the time, there is an amplification of who we authentically are. The seasons indicate a change in position.

There is always a change of guard. I served in the military for many years, and I will always remember guard duty. When I lived in Sinai, Egypt, the base was guarded 24/7, and there was always a shift change. With each new set of eyes, everyone brought their own perspective, but they all had the same goal: to keep people safe. That means regardless of the rank of the individual in the position, the level of authority given was the same simply because they were in that position. For this base, they had guard towers.

God created the sea, animals, etc., before man, but it was humans who became the dominant ones, the ones to rule. However, creation still plays its role and tells us how to treat it during specific seasons. For example, when it is hot in many places in the U.S., it is common for there to be a heavy downpour of rain to saturate the ground because the earth is too dry. Therefore, creation positions itself to provide the rain. The rain droplets form a cloud, and when they are gathered to full capacity, the cloud releases water from the sky. Every element must align itself to produce. In a season when life seems to release rain, we can look at it as we are being positioned to produce. The cloud is fully aware of what it is created to do. It knows when it reaches a certain level, it is time to release, to pour out. God knows when we are ready to pour out, but do we?

How to Break Habits That Create Obscurity In Your Vision and Fog Up Your Awareness

Because we are creatures of habit, it is required to be present when we learn to release—release elements that no longer have a purpose. Yes, when we were younger or simply in a different place in life, we created ways to cope, deal, and survive. But now the goal is to live in full thriving mode, staying in moments and purging yourself of the thoughts that constantly tell us to escape. That was me; it was easy to leave. Then, it became a consistent part of my life while I was in the military. We moved every four years, so if there were issues you did not want to face, it was easy to leave. That is a habit I found myself continuing to dictate the pattern of my life. I am grateful for what I call the process of developing well. Notice the word process.

Many times, it has been said that everything has a process. How do we know what the process is? It's simple. The process is what it takes to get to what or where you want to be. Going from the place where you are, whether that be mentally or physically, we are all in a state of mind. We should stop here, and if we do nothing else, let us ask ourselves, what state is my mind in? Am I holding on to things I cannot control? Is there something physical stopping me from breaking cycles that do not serve me? The biggest issue with this scenario is not only do they not serve me, but the ability to serve me is gone. The realization is that this thing has reached its maximum usage in my life and no longer produces anything viable for me to develop well.

I was having a conversation with a friend, and what I gathered from it was that no matter how old we get, that is not the determining factor as to whether we develop well. Developing well, simply put, is thriving. BUT (Believers Understanding Truth) know to thrive means there are old habits that must be broken and made to stop while at the same time creating new habits to replace the empty space. We can only do this if we are present, intentional, and willing. The process consists of the steps we are willing to take to achieve it. As we develop on the journey, the climb increases. The creativity of thought causes us to go further than we have ever gone. Stay open to ask questions. Questions break old habits. When we accept a new way of thinking or, better yet, expand our thoughts, we are choosing to become well-developed.

In the beginning, the questions may have made us discount the value of who we are. It is not just outsiders who consistently question, but the person looking in the mirror every day. BUT the more we ask, the more the discovery of our endless potential. Asking questions brings the opportunity to gain experience and grow. The more we ask, the more we know. The understanding of the homo sapiens is revealed with each answer. Life will verify the information from the right source, and we will know because there will be growth.

It has given, and is giving, insight to humanity that is ready to become the phenomenon of today. Questions help us express the information we seek and provide the direction to pursue it. Therefore, developing questioning skills is a crucial part of learning and thinking deeply and critically about who we are. Making a request of yourself is crucial for self-awareness. Eliciting information about yourself should bring helpful answers to use as guidance in the course of life.

What is the Process?

A process is a sequence of steps that occur over time. I hope our intent is to achieve a result or reach a goal. A process may be planned and unplanned. A process that is planned by humans for a purpose is the course of action taken or a procedure to reach an end product.

First, before anything, we must know what we are looking to achieve. But we must be willing to ask questions. This is the only way we will get the right outcome. Sometimes, we have to sit in a posture of meditation, quieting all voices when seeking answers, making sure to listen and not push off what we predetermine is something out of our reach. Be present always; this will put you in a state of openness. This is not a comfortable place because we have experienced hurt, disappointment, and pain at some point during our lives. There are times in the past when we may have allowed emotions that challenged us to make us stand still or get stuck in the negatively charged emotion. Remember, being vulnerable and open to hearing can make us uncomfortable. Now, the awareness of being uncomfortable is there. Use the emotion to push through to the other side where you want to live, in the abundance of fulfilling your purpose.

Whenever we feel something that is not good, there is always a positive to a negative. Leif Garrett said, "I've come to understand that there's always something positive, even in a negative situation." Things we must work through always build strength, endurance, and stamina. Now, if we choose not to put in the effort to go through that, a growth opportunity is missed. If you are in a situation that you feel is keeping you stuck, I need you to see yourself on the other side. I need you to find where the opening is in you. Ask the necessary questions that give insight into this part of the process and instruct you on how to keep moving forward. Even if it is a minuscule step, it is still a step, and tomorrow, you will commit to taking another step. Go ahead and ask yourself a question. Open up and do a self-inventory, or better yet, an analysis, an observation of you.

In Corinthians, Paul gives instructions on what to do before we come to the Lord's table and partake in the act of remembrance, acknowledging that Jesus has removed the wall of separation from us and God. So, when we remember all that was accomplished for us, knowing the steps are in place for us to do everything here on earth that God has given us to do, we recognize that this is part of the process. Yes, examining our motives and evaluating our hearts is a crucial part of the process. We know when we are doing something for the wrong reasons.

The process of seeing something or someone carefully or gaining information helps us continue on the journey. In this case, we are looking to learn our own ways. Then, we do our best to drop the patterns that cause us to falter. People are kept in the hospital for observation. Doctors gain information on how to help the patient through watching. Observation allows us to respond to life in a suitable manner. Instead of losing our temper quickly after seeing our behavior, we begin to make strides to respond and not react. We do not want to move so fast that what we do causes this ripple effect of negativity.

Unfortunately, the only person who is going to ultimately reap the benefit of the negativity is you. As we take our series of steps in navigating life and making sure we stay present, it is important we learn to respond. This means we are careful, thoughtful listeners and speakers who carefully choose words and are slow to anger. We pride ourselves on being patient, reflective, and forgiving of others and ourselves. When we live with this principle, we are just about guaranteed to be successful.

How do I know? Well, there is truth to the saying, "When we know better, we do better." Knowing who we are, I mean our true self, not the person we show others. When we are not sure of who we are. We can only do better when we know what is not good about us. When we take the time to examine ourselves, all our senses get involved. This is what enables us to do better. Now, the body can execute. In the last paragraph of my book *"Don't Let Your Brain Go Numb: Regaining Power Through Resilience,"* it says, "The caveat to this is, your mind – the center of everything within you, must be active and alive so it can provide instructions to your heart and your heart will give instructions to your body and your body will execute the command." If we are going to receive commands for the body to execute, first, what we tell our mind must come from a place of being better and doing better. This is one of the challenging areas of being present because we are our own watchdog. We watch what we say; we watch what we are doing when life shows up. When it does, we ensure that we have been practicing through listening and choosing our words wisely so as not to harm or destroy ourselves or anyone else in the process. We must also ensure there is no room for uncontrolled tempers, that we are not derailed, and that we are able to stay in the moment, still being calm, peaceful, and loving always. Getting to this point and staying consistently here is this state of mind that requires us to make changes in multiple areas of life. BUT (Believers Understanding Truth) know that the most important thing is to have our hearts changed, renewed, and recharged on a regular basis.

For us to maneuver as smoothly as possible through life effectively, we need great observation skills and must continually examine ourselves. Observation will give you all the information you need to live free, and when you are free, no one or nothing can confine, paralyze, or restrain you. Paying attention and being present in every moment takes away thoughts that will lead to limited thinking. BUT we are equipped to overcome false thoughts by simply being willing.

Willingness

The question is: are you willing? Do you crave with a deep desire to achieve greatness? Not material wealth but having the ability to possess a mindset where no matter what, the way is upward thinking. A pattern of thought focused on ascension and never in a direction of descent.

Willingness opens doors and provides opportunities. Willingness and opportunity equal readiness. When I served in the Army, everyone had to maintain readiness status. If you were not able to sustain the level of skill needed, you were not a benefit to them. Now, I know you may not have served in the military; however, we have all been in uncomfortable situations. Life brings those moments around every now and then. Insert a smile here; a smile is needed for encouragement to keep reading. You are almost at the end of the book, and the area of willingness is a key ingredient to success. So, I wanted to give you a boost to show you that you can push yourself to a place of willingness—with a smile.

When we find ourselves in uncomfortable positions, it is necessary to be prepared with willingness. You may not have everything you need physically at that moment, BUT if you are willing, the things you need will find you.

Have you ever been in a position where you had to make a phone call you did not want to make? Then, it turns out the outcome was amenable once you showed your willingness to cooperate and acknowledge your role. Not just for the person you called but for you too.

Now, let's look at it like this. Willingness causes us to become ready speedily; we are prepared with eagerness and keen awareness. Being keenly aware affords us the opportunity to think quickly. The skill of thinking quickly and soundly brings the creative life-giving side from within to the forefront of your mind. Doing it innately is the goal. Daily, we should create by bringing out our inherent character. Without the display of the essential parts of who we are, it is impossible to reach our full potential.

In Isaiah 1:19, the Amplified translation says, "If you are willing and obedient, you shall eat the best of the land." Willingness requires obedience—obedience to God. Oh yes, there is work to be done. BUT (Believers Understanding Truth), the land does not produce if no work is done to it. The word is straightforward on this. "If you do not work, you do not eat." If you expect to yield a harvest while on earth, then start working—not necessarily a 9-5, but working on that thing you were created to leave here.

The Greek word "ergon" means to work until something is accomplished. There is an action that produces evidence of the things we hoped for. We are the land that must produce. God gave us the power to create when he breathed the breath of life into us.

NEWS FLASH: Every day we wake up, our breath is supplied. It is up to you and me to use this life-achieving breath to make dreams manifest and make them become tangible. This book you are reading, whether it is paperback or electronic, you are now partaking of what this land produced. As you eat the good things from the land, you will readily generate fruit. There will be evidence of God living through you. At all costs, you must produce "love, joy, peace, patience, kindness, goodness, faithfulness, gentleness, and self-control."

***2 Thessalonians 3:10 (The Message Translation)** - Don't you remember the rule we had when we lived with you? "If you don't work, you don't eat."*

Acknowledgment

Acknowledgment requires a response. This may take effort because sometimes we are responding to something we do not fully understand at that moment. This brings a point to the forefront. We do not have to have specific instructions for every step we are taking, but it is necessary to acknowledge we are taking steps. These are steps of faith, believing that God is leading the way. These steps are already planned out. Our responsibility is to trust the process.

Being present will allow us to recognize growth and identify the need to cultivate this space of awareness. As we expand and deepen our mindfulness, everything about us becomes devoted to who we are. Then, our responsiveness to life will change. Here is where we are in a continuous flow of living in peace. Being present opens us to a place of peace and understanding that life is not the enemy. Now, things may not be in perfect order right now, but keep responding with confessions of confident words that construct positive outcomes. Yes, you can do that. When negative things happen, or thoughts come, acknowledge them too. This is a clear sign you are present in the moment, but that does not mean you must accept it. You are such a powerful being, and you can change your perspective of what is happening.

Our views will dictate our behavior, and our behavior will solidify what we think. This means what we believe will be the outcome or the product of how life appears. Think about what you are thinking about. Mindfulness—the presence of awareness—is needed to monitor and control our thoughts. Our thinking influences our emotions, which affect our behavior and choices. By cultivating a positive mindset, challenging negative thoughts, and harnessing the power of visualization, we can take control of our lives and create a more fulfilling future.

Once we accept what we willingly acknowledge, adjusting to become aligned with purpose is so much easier. Perhaps not always without ease, but we are able to accomplish life goals while being calm and at peace. Always having the understanding that just because things are not feeling the best does not dictate the presence of peace. As we acknowledge our own existence here on earth, it should produce constant prompting and encourage us to seek self-actualization.

Self-actualization is when we are fully satisfied with how we produce what we can fulfill at that time. I believe there are many times of self-actualization as we are on a persistent quest to improve as humans who are driven to be a vital force in this world. We cannot just lay back and be idle and think that we will become. There is effort that goes into fulfillment. Acknowledgment opens the door to direction. It is easy to follow when we recognize the way we are going is the best for us. I can feel the excitement build as I reflect on the day I accepted who I am. Knowing that you have gifts and talents to share with the world should set your mind in a high state of feeling loved and valued. Not because anyone told you but because you believe in yourself and your capabilities. Oh, what a wonderful mindset.

Of course, there will be times when you feel you have no clue what you're doing, but as long as you keep reaching and striving, doors will open, and "your gift will make room for you." As Dr. Myles Munroe once said, "Your gift will make way for you in life. It is in exercising this gift that you will find real fulfillment, purpose, and contentment in your work," referencing Proverbs 18:16. Your movement towards goals is evidence you believe, and I hope you are at a point of trust. Trust you and your competencies. Believing that you deserve the best things in life is your superpower.

Proverbs 3:6 (New International Version) - in all your ways submit to him, and he will make your paths straight.

Proverbs 3:6 (New Living Translation) - Seek his will in all you do, and he will show you which path to take.

Proverbs 3:6 (English Standard Version) - In all your ways acknowledge him, and he will make straight your paths.

Adjustments

Big or small, life will require alterations of our behaviors, which will create our desire to grow and develop on a consistent basis. However, in the event we choose to decline growth for whatever reason, know that you will continue to stay in the same place. Often, that is literally a physical place, but the good news is we were not created to be stagnant. What do you see when you see the word stagnant? When was the last time you saw a human who was motionless, immobile, inactive? Exactly, unless you were at a funeral yesterday (and if you were, my condolences). But if you were not, then you understand a human should always be being.

Making life happen, not the other way around, just allowing life to happen. Oh no! We are continuously moving, living, and having our being. Because you are breathing, these words apply to you. Moving means making progress, focusing, refocusing, transforming, and influencing. When we create movement in our lives, things begin to change, and vision is needed to be successful in our movements. As we grow in the stewardship of life and become responsible for managing the gifts we embody, it is key to be wise and mature in our thoughts. Living in a consistent state of effectively adjusting to who we are comes with influence. There will always be a level of influence when we are willing to transform the way we think and act.

Ephesians 4:21-25 (Amplified Bible) - ²¹ *If in fact, you have [really] heard Him and have been taught by Him, just as truth is in Jesus [revealed in His life and personified in Him], ²² regarding your previous way of life, you put off your old self [completely discard your former nature], which is being corrupted through deceitful desires, ²³ and be continually renewed in the spirit of your mind [having a fresh, untarnished mental and spiritual attitude], ²⁴ and put on the new self [the regenerated and renewed nature], created in God's image, [godlike] in the righteousness and holiness of the truth [living in a way that expresses to God your gratitude for your salvation]. ²⁵ Therefore, rejecting all falsehood [whether lying, defrauding, telling half-truths, spreading rumors, any such as these], speak truth each one with his neighbor, for we are all parts of one another [and we are all parts of the body of Christ].*

The act of transforming our minds creates a renewal of how we think, and it is then that we can easily adjust our mental and spiritual attitudes. It is here we will have our being. Being is only in the now. It is impossible to have being at any other moment than now. At your present now, you are being a sponge, soaking in nutrients from the expression of thought that fills these pages. Stay soft and light, porous, not to things that distract, detract, or disempower you, but to the truth. Always be free to express your gratitude to God for making all things in your life untarnished and for experiencing a life full of great discoveries about who we are.

Alignments

There is nothing more exhilarating than to be spiritually, mentally, and physically aligned with yourself as the creation—a living, breathing, moving creation that is on a continual cycle of goodness and mercy. That provides us opportunities to expand far beyond what our eyes can see. This is why we must stay laser-focused on where we are in life. The key is to be determined to envision every moment as sacred and holy. No, not religious, but in the sanctity of what is set apart for you at that specific time.

In every moment, there are opportunities to grow spiritually; as a spirit being, this must be understood, not avoided. Embrace your spirit. What is it saying to you in this very moment? This moment will take you to your next; there is no rush. The moment is now. Be in it. Feel it. Learn it. Learn from it. Your being is gaining wisdom for what is needed to stay in your continual cycle of goodness and mercy. Just like our spirit, we cannot see them, but we know they are there, bringing in all things for our good and providing endless mercy to last through whatever! Whew, did you feel the excitement? I had to put an exclamation point for emphasis there. This is where I coined the phrase, "I am an outlaster of all my pain." It is not in the dictionary yet, but I speak it will be! Again, exclaiming to create excitement through the expression of thought being poured out. I am ecstatic to share my heart with you. The intent is to always ignite and build.

Alignment is "the arrangement in a straight line, or in correct or appropriate position."

Selah

Let that sink in. When I read that on the Microsoft Office top results, I had to stop because it hit me that there was a stipulation here. If you intend to be in alignment, you must also be willing to be arranged and put in the required order. Now is where we must make a cognizant choice. Going in with full awareness of the outcome that our lives will change in some way. There is a requirement for you as the creation. Hopefully, this next statement will ease any sense of anxiety. Being willing and obedient is part of the requirement to eat the good of the land (Isaiah 1:19). Be a participant in your life. Having daily experiences of the abundance of good health, good relationships, influence, and peace of mind. That is what alignment looks like. BUT (Believers Understanding Truth) know there is a guided process for this. Next time things feel out of sorts, understand that it is key for positioning. Your thoughts will dictate whether you follow the right guide. Thoughts that keep you in the present. Thoughts of your future is God's business. It is our business to believe in the hope that was given to us so we can reach the future. Being and becoming our best self spiritually, emotionally, and physically. Your now is guiding you to your future, but it is not the future we are focusing on; it is the present moment that is here for a purpose, and we cannot afford to miss its "why."

Being present gives you reference points in time. Your point in time is when you decide to make your point. Choose to make your qualities known.

There is a knowing when you understand your gift, and with that knowing comes a better understanding. There is a requirement to be present when you are aware of your gifting. I was just thinking about one of mine: The gift of empathy. When we are empathic people, most likely, this becomes evident in how we deal with people and how we can understand them because of the knowledge that we have within ourselves.

Being aligned helps us to pay attention. Concentrating on the call of God is extremely important. Today was one of those moments when I was about to allow my body to dictate what I was going to do next. BUT (Believers Understanding Truth) know the call is louder when we have taken the hours, months, days, and years to train our hearing. The call causes you to spring forth. Have you ever had a moment when you begin to move towards who you are without hesitation? You freely flow toward the present that is calling. However, because you are in the present, the observation from within shows you, you. The authenticity of who you are stands up. It raises a standard against anything wanting to stop you from answering the call.

Let me elaborate. I was lying in bed on a Sunday morning. It's a beautiful gray day, and my body and mind begin to speak, giving suggestions like, "Oh, go ahead, just lay in the bed..." giving instructions that would lead to nothing. Then, as I lay there, words begin to erupt in my heart, and I automatically know the sound. I know the voice; yes, it is my own voice, but the vibration of the sound comes through differently when it grips your soul. You see, my soul resonates with this sound because it is calling to my place of passion, and one of them is writing. Here is where I needed to make a choice. Follow the sound, answer the call, or just lay there. You are a witness that I answered, and here are the words that erupted from my soul.

"Yes, here! Present and accounted for." We used to say these words at every roll call. I began to ask questions right away. What does that mean for today? Because it came back to me for a reason. I know my gift; it would not have come to me if there were not going to be an explanation. While pondering, praying, and meditating on these words, I thought of how they apply to everyday life because we need clarity for everyday life.

Here is my take. When I was in the military, we said this, or the leader of the squad would give this report during morning formations. There were times when the leader would say, "Two missing...all others accounted for." Now, that was someone providing an answer for a group. Giving the impression that this group is ready to fulfill that day's mission. For an individual to answer for a group, they must believe that who and what they see at that moment indicates to him or her that everyone is equipped to do their part. This account is ascertained by vision. The person on the outside has no clue that there could be factors of distraction roaming through the minds of individuals under their leadership.

I digress for a moment. While serving as a leader, I was given the gift of compassion, which is a key trait of being a great leader. This gave me the ability to establish a rapport with those I served. One day, I had a conversation with one of my superiors with the intent of helping her guide those of us she was charged to lead. I said, "Don't let me come here one day, and the MPs (military police) are here because you have barricaded yourself in your office with one of the younger troops having lost it on you." Now, here is some background. She was responsible for 25 troops at the time, and 13 of them were under the age of 25 and grew up in various parts of the country, all in an urban setting. The leader was a Caucasian woman who had not had this experience and needed a little training in speaking to others with tact. Please understand that I trusted she never had ill will towards any of us; she just did not have the experience.

I wanted to see her succeed as a leader because she did have a genuine heart. I said to her, "You never know what they faced before getting to work." As I mentioned, they were very young, and their limited experience in life did not provide them with the wisdom they needed to navigate life. For some, they had wives and babies, trying to live on a salary that was not enough to maintain a household in a large metropolitan area. Therefore, depending on how she spoke to them, it could be good or bad, and I was there to ensure that it would go well. I can say that now, as many years have passed, reflection lets me know that there was always a purpose of good for wherever I was stationed. It worked. Not only did she change her way of communication with us, but several years later, I was promoted to Staff Sergeant, and she sent me a message; I believe we had email by this time (insert laugh here). The message said, "If anyone deserves this, it is you." She remembered the conversation we had, and she expressed her appreciation as it had helped her grow as a leader. She had gone on to rise high in rank.

So, I digressed to illustrate that I believe it is impossible for another person to affirm someone else's state of accountability. Yes, because of eyesight, we can unequivocally say someone is physically in a state of mind. BUT we can only take responsibility for our accountability. The soldiers I spoke of earlier might have been distracted because of external circumstances, which is something that no one is immune to. These agitations would be difficult for anyone, but especially for someone who did not have life experiences that would give them the wisdom to focus on the mission.

Now, you are really going to get a chuckle out of this. Our mission was to provide dental service to 1000-plus troops on the base. Okay, now that you are no longer laughing, this is a very important supportive mission. The dental field is a skill that requires you to score high on your military entry exam. That said, although the soldiers were from what is considered urban, they were intelligent beings. If we were not in place to make sure everyone was up to date with their dental health, it could certainly cause a problem if they were in extreme pain trying to save the life of a country.

I answered the call of my gift to write this morning to help us understand the importance of being not just physically present but, more importantly, taking accountability for our presence. Taking accountability means being responsible for managing our lives. We cannot take for granted the gifts we have been given by not answering them. Being obedient to who you are is not always easy, and I did not encourage my former leader to be soft on the guys, just respectful, because that is the responsibility of any leader.

I hope these words bring clarity to being present, and I love the usage of this connector here and *accounted* for. We must be more than physically present. Our presence should be connected to a demonstration that our behavior is representative of what I call our reasonable service—that thing we bring to earth that makes us answerable to who we are.

It is the *and* for me. Being present and accounted for is "when each part [with power adapted to its need] is working properly [in all its functions], grows to full maturity, building itself up in love" (later part of Ephesians 4:16, Amplified Version). Presence comes with the power to do your part, and we continue to grow in wisdom so that we can conduct our lives by showing responsibility and accountability.

So, I must ask, are you present and accounted for?

Made in the USA
Middletown, DE
04 September 2024